All About Plant

T0080665

All About

Flowers

Claire Throp

CAPSTONE PRESS
a capstone imprint

© 2015 Heinemann Library
an imprint of Capstone Global Library, LLC
Chicago, Illinois

All rights reserved. No part of this publication may be reproduced or transmitted in any form or by any means, electronic or mechanical, including photocopying, recording, taping, or any information storage and retrieval system, without permission in writing from the publisher.

Edited by Claire Throp and Brynn Baker
Designed by Peggie Carley
Picture research by Ruth Blair
Production by Victoria Fitzgerald
Originated by Capstone Global Library Ltd

Library of Congress Cataloging-in-Publication Data

ISBN 978-1-4846-0506-6 (hardcover)
ISBN 978-1-4846-3846-0 (paperback)
ISBN 978-1-4846-0512-7 (ebook PDF)

Acknowledgments

We would like to thank the following for permission to reproduce photographs:

Getty Images: Andrew Dernie, cover; iStockphoto: srebrina, 9 (left); Shutterstock: Anna Omelchenko, 12, 23 (middle), Artens, 9 (right), Birdiegal, 20 (left), Butterfly Hunter, 20 (right), Charles Brutlag, 22, Eduardo Ramirez Sanchez, 21, Elena Elisseeva, 8, Filipe B. Varela, 5, Frank L. Junior, 14, freya-photographer, 13, Habitus, 19, Jorge Salcedo, 16, Kenneth Keifer, 17, Kostex, 11, loreanto, 15, 23 (top), Pavelk, 6, Sompoch Tangthai, back cover, 18, Stefan Holm, 4, Yevgeniy Steshkin, 10, 23 (bottom), Yuriy Kulik, 7

We would like to thank Michael Bright for his invaluable help in the preparation of this book.

Every effort has been made to contact copyright holders of material reproduced in this book. Any omissions will be rectified in subsequent printings if notice is given to the publisher.

Contents

What Are Plants?

Plants are living things.

flower

stem

leaf

root

seed

Plants have
many parts.

What Do Plants Need to Grow?

Plants need water to grow.

Plants need sunlight
and air to grow.

What Are Flowers?

Many plants grow flowers.

Some plants have one flower.
Some plants have lots of flowers.

Flowers make **seeds**.

New plants grow from seeds.

Petals

petal

A **petal** is one part of a flower.

Some flowers have purple petals.

Some flowers have red petals.

Some flowers have **patterns**
on their petals.

Shapes

Flowers can be different shapes.
Some flowers look like a ball.

Some flowers look like a heart.

Some flowers look like a star.

Some flowers look like a bell.

Flowers as Food

Hummingbirds and butterflies
get food from flowers.

Bees get food from flowers.

Plants Need Flowers

seed

Flowers make seeds. Seeds grow
and become new plants.

Picture Glossary

pattern colors, shapes, or lines that are repeated

petal part of a flower that is often bright in color

seed part of a plant that new plants grow from

Index

Notes for Parents and Teachers

Before Reading

Gather together a variety of flowers or photos of flowers. Ask children to describe each, including its color and shape. If you have actual flowers, have children smell them. Ask children why they think flowers smell and why some have colorful patterns (to attract insects and some birds)

After Reading

- Ask children why insects and birds are neccessary for plants to survive. How do insects and birds help plants?
- Have children draw a flower from the book and label the flower's parts, such as the petals, roots, and stem.
- Have children work with partners to describe the flowers in the book. One child describes the flower's color, pattern, or shape, and the other child finds the flower in the book. The children switch roles.